Naked Prayers

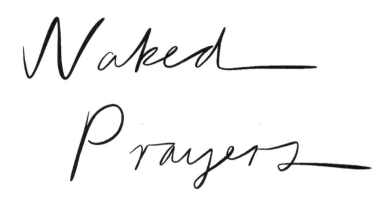

Naked Prayers

honest confessions
to a loving creator

by
Mara Measor

elevate

For permission requests, please address
Elevate Publishing

Published by Elevate Publishing, Boise, ID
ISBN-13: 978-1937498306

Content

Naked Prayers

is a book and album project.

Every time you see this symbol on a page:

there is a song accompanying the prayer.

Enjoy the music that was written
alongside this book by visiting
nakedprayers.com

Thank you for being a part of this story!

But when you pray, go into your room and shut the door and pray to your Father who is in secret.

Matthew 6:6

For it sufficeth enough, a naked intent unto God without any other cause than Himself.

The Cloud of Unknowing

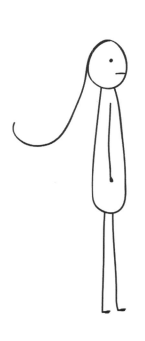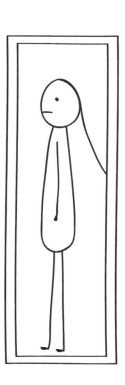

From the editor

Good girls don't pray on street corners.

Well, I do, sometimes, like earlier today
on Waverly and Sixth —
not to be seen by men. In silence I was thanking God,
who gives and gives good gifts.

Thank you for the shoes I used to get to Caffe Reggio.
Thank you for money to treat a friend to cappuccino.
Thank you for the lamplight that made my way home safe.
Thank you for the Bible waiting on my bed.

I feast on a trail of crumbs and of letters.

Bianca van der Meulen

Intro

Most of us start our days by putting on layers of clothing. Underwear, shirt, pants, a jacket. Maybe some makeup for the ladies, and hair gel (wax? pomade?) for the men. To that, we add the smiles and the mannerisms that mark our carefully constructed individuality and the endless other layers we protect, perfect, and puff ourselves up with.

I don't remember a time before my consciousness of God's presence in my life. As a girl, I just knew He was there. As I got older though, I began relying on everyone else's version of who God is and how to be a good Christian. My knowledge of Him grew but so, too, did my distance from Him. I knew far more what other people said about Him than what I knew of Him myself, and that made me behave strangely in our time together. Like dressing for a repeated first date, I would put on my best to speak to my maker. Fully clothed and carefully made up, I would speak politely. I spoke like someone I imagined God would like to hear from, who knew all the right ways to pray and glittered with holiness.

But I'm me. My sentences are not particularly elegant; I like doodling more than doctrine; I am small and sometimes weak.

I knew God for many years before I started suspecting He might prefer that I speak to Him as I was, oafishness galore. But during the year I spent in Ethiopia when no one else around me seemed to understand a word I said — I turned to God in a new way. I spoke to Him as though he was actually in my room. In the little town I was living with only enough water supply for me to shower twice a week, my outer appearance floundered but my inner life blossomed. I started to strip away the layers and really talk to my God. With honesty and simplicity, I told Him about my desires and dreams. I looked into my mirror and talked to Him about what I saw.

It was a grand experiment, and I wanted to see where it would go. So I started to write my prayers down. Maybe, over time, I would get a little older and a little wiser in the way I related to Him. Maybe I could give Him a little more room to relate back to me.

Five years passed. The year was 2012. I didn't know it then, but the journey that became Naked Prayers was about to begin. I was fresh out of college, full of ideas about who I was and what God wanted of me. Pain was not reflecting in the mirror.

I always thought having depression meant feeling a bit sad a bit too often. I learned better. Like those who have struggled before me and those who are struggling now, I watched my sunny world turn a frightening shade of dark. Over the 14 months recorded in these prayers, as I fought to make a home in New York City and support my family in crisis in Hong Kong, I lost all direction and purpose. I pushed blindly through each day. I bought groceries, performed on stage, had coffee with my friends. But I was in hiding. I hid from everyone, except God.

Like in Ethiopia, once again it seemed He was the only one who could understand me. The only one who would not be afraid of the depth of darkness in which I lay.

As I began my emotional free fall, following Him seemed impossible. Yet I see now that a hand was always stretched out to catch me. As I exposed my heart to God, He responded. I don't know how else to explain the presence of scripture in my prayers and in this book. Sometimes, halfway through a prayer, a verse would come to mind. Other times, my whole prayer was a response to a verse that spoke to me on a certain day. But, much more often than I realized, my own words evoked passages I wasn't even conscious of. God's voice formed the basis of almost every praise and plea. In the delight of discovery, I have exposed these hidden verses in the book's final pages. It makes me smile to know that truly, the same spirit has been leading men to pray since the time of Genesis.

We all need someone to speak for us sometimes. The Spirit Himself intercedes for us with groanings too deep for words. This is especially true when we're going through pain that leaves us dumbfounded, but it's also true when we feel tired, lonely, or just uninspired. This is not a how-to-pray book, but a how-I-have-really-prayed book. While my prayers can't instruct you, hopefully they can offer the assurance that you're not alone, forgotten, or unheard, even (especially) when you don't know what to say.

There's no right way to read this book. Read through the pages in one sitting. Set the book on your bedside table (or, if you are like me, on the pile of clothes beside your bed) and read whichever page you happen to flip to on a given night. Go straight to the fourth section, Finding, to get a quick shot of comfort. Use these prayers in whatever way emboldens you to wipe the dust off your own mirror and get naked before your maker. May they welcome you into a quiet place where you have the freedom to be fully yourself before God.

October 2012

A year ago, I graduated from college. I am one of the lucky ones; I was cast in an Off-Broadway production a month out of school, and now I have a manager and an agent sending me out to parts of New York I thought were reserved exclusively for important people. On top of that, a producer who had heard my original songs through a workshop I did had approached me, interested in signing me to his label. I said, "Yes, please!"

Recently though, my family had not been one of the lucky ones. My dearest father had a stroke, then pneumonia, and through an unfortunate incident at the hospital, dislocated his leg and became permanently bed-bound. I went to be with him. My dad occupies a deeply special place right by the center of my heart, and the series of events had made a little dent inside me. At the time, I was torn up about returning to America. But each time I asked my dad whether or not I should stay back in Hong Kong with him, he would firmly shake his head no. He wanted me to pursue my dreams.

I don't know what my dreams are, but I have a great desire to create beautiful things. I want to affect strangers with my acting and my music. And since New York, the land of arts and strangers, seemed to be beckoning me with open arms, I listened to my dad and made my way back into the neon jungle.

I want to prove to my family that my work here is worth the separation. I was just granted a work visa as an Alien of Extraordinary Abilities (no, I didn't make that up), and I am nervous but giddy-excited about the album I am recording. Here is my chance to surprise everyone with what Little Mara can do.

I'm stretched a little thin. I work two part-time jobs beside the recording and occasional acting projects. But my faith is a spring beneath my feet bouncing me forward so I can keep in pace with how darned quickly people move here. I believe God is with me, I believe He has placed me in New York for a grand purpose, and I believe he will guide me forward.

My prayer is to be a devoted follower, eyes glued on my loving maker.

October 19

John the Baptist knew his purpose so clearly. He was so
streamlined.
I think his simple lifestyle blessed him with clarity.[1]

Lord, living in a busy city clouds my vision. So many things
everywhere . . . The moment I don't know where I'm going,
I get tugged and pulled in all these different directions. I get
overwhelmed.

I think sometimes I act like everything is up to me.
Like everything is in my control and I have to figure it all out
on my own.
And you're just watching or something.

I know that's silly. My life never belonged to me — I am yours. You bought me with a price. A painful price. A price I don't ever want to forget, even though I do over and over and over . . .

You gave your son to make me your child.
You are my father.
Help me to remember!

I want to be clearly moving toward you.
I want to remember that I am yours. Yours.
    Touched by you.
    Sustained by you.

May I be more like John the Baptist! May I follow you more simply. A little more honey and locusts, a little less processed sugar and genetically modified chicken.

October 20

Father, I trust you!
Let your will always be done.
Your ways are perfect.[1] I am confident in that.
You are a good God, and you are good to me.
Gentle and loving, you hold my heart.

All I am,
all I know,
all I want,
all I fear,
all I need, I give to you.
(Well, I'm trying.)

In my life,
in all things,
at all times,
let it be as you say.

I will lie down tonight in peace, knowing that you will
continue to sing over me.
Forgive me, Lord, when I forget you.

October 21

Sometimes it's easier to talk to you with a pen in my hand. I see the pen. I see the prayer. I know what they are or what I am doing.

God, you're so big, so mysterious.
You like to use the foolish to shame the wise . . .[1]
May I be the kind of fool you love.

Love me!

Go with me where I go.
I never want to turn my face from you.
Will you show me the things I don't know?

October 22

My future is decreed by you, Lord.
My every step is determined by you, not by any human.[1]
You write my story, no one else.

I will not be overwhelmed.
I will not be a flower tossed by the waves.[2]
I will not be sucked into the things that pass away.

I love you more than all of that.

no . . .

October 24

I just realized, here, on this train, that it's actually illogical for me to despair about anything, knowing who you are. Hope is real when the maker of the universe cared enough for me to give his own son for my freedom.

The Lord is my light and my salvation;
whom shall I fear?
The Lord is the stronghold of my life;
of whom shall I be afraid?

Psalm 27:1

Answer: Nobody.
Help me to remember that!

I like being on trains. You keep moving, though all you have to do is sit. I think that's how it feels to live in the spirit.

Holy Spirit, you are my train. I pray I will sit in you every day!

October 30

For our God is a consuming fire.

Hebrews 12:29

A consuming fire swallows everything in its path. It is awesome. It is mighty.
Have I been consumed by your fire, Lord?
Or do I let an old flame sustain my dim light?

How do you see me right now, God?
I want to see how you see.

Sometimes I forget that you want to love me.
I forget that you delight in your love for me.
I forget that it pleases you when I laugh.
That you sing over me when I weep.

I am so forgetful!
I forget that, with you, I can't possibly be alone.
That angels follow at my call.
That Jesus picks me up as I fall.

I'm sorry that I forget these things when, really, I want to
remember you. I want to see you in my dreams, in my
thoughts. I want to remember what you did, what you do
for me.

Today I walked around and realized you are even bigger
than I thought yesterday.

November 2

Father? Draw near to me.

Feels like there's pollution inside me.
I don't know what I'm doing.
I want someone (you, Lord, you) to tell me something to
calm my fears.

Cleanse me, God — white as snow would be nice.[1]

November 4

Teach me how to pray for my daddy.

I want him to find you, meet you, surrender to you. I pray, God, that each night as he sleeps he will experience the loving arms of his saviour. I want you to speak to his bones and breathe new life into him. For the sake of your love for your children, for the sake of your fatherhood, let the remainder of my daddy's days be a reflection of your goodness and faithfulness. Wipe away every tear, melt his fears by your love, and hold him ever near. Hold him. I want him to know he is held by you. Prepare him for eternity with you. For the sake of your glory, call to this precious child and father. I believe in your will. And I know you want him in your arms. Show him where you are, and help him to make his way there.

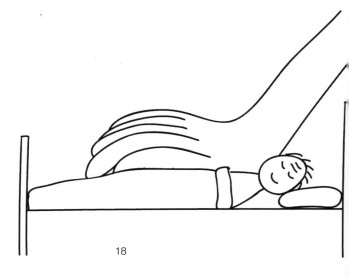

I pray for the people you have placed in my life, including my family. Bind us together in love. Truth. Let your truth penetrate our stubbornness. I confess our pride, how we each feel to be in the right, in the light, and we forget that we are all utterly dependent on You always, always, always.

November 10

Father. Hi.
Today I am Gideon, sitting under a tree.[1]
Will you visit me?
I wouldn't dream of smashing idols on my own, but I'm very
interested in a partnership with you.

I want to hold your finger.
I want to wrap myself around your thumb.
I don't mind hanging there a bit.
Lord, reveal your breathing rate to me.

November 23

Lord, I'm learning to turn to you more and more and more.
It's nice.

My ambitions.
Lift them from me and refine them, please.
Take them.
Break them.
Bless them.
Then give them back.

I'm with you, God.
I will have peace with your pace.
Take your time with me.

I know I'm stubborn, and I want to keep busy,
busy, busy.
Please speak to me and slow me down.
Make me into a listener, and
let your voice be my path!

November 24

If their purpose or activity is of human origin, it will fail. But if it is from God, you will not be able to stop these men.

Acts 5:38-39 (NIV)

That is so exciting. But I'm afraid so far I've been very stoppable.

May the things I do fall into that latter category!
May I find a purpose and activities that are of heavenly origin, so I become an unstoppable extension of you, Lord!

November 29

Soften me, Father.

My heart is hardening. I don't quite know how, I just feel it.
I'm going my own way. I'm anxious for myself.
For my future.
For my present.
For my family.

I've been a poor friend to you.

Father, I'm so impatient to be doing good things. Good
things that are obvious to me and the people around me,
so I can be obviously seen as a good person. I get sucked
into my own definitions, and I pursue whatever I define
worthy in the moment, regardless of your voice.

I haven't been good to you.
I haven't been faithful in the little things.
I don't want to be this way.

Forgive me.

December 2

I'm seeing more and more clearly that I need discipline every day of my life. I need to develop spiritual workout routines to build my strength in you.[1] I want this even though workouts never feel good, and I won't see the results right away,

I want to be disciplined.

I know very well I will trip and fall as I climb these stairs, but I think worse would be not to climb at all.

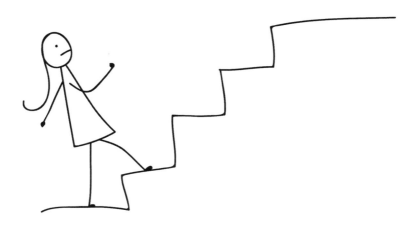

December 7

Pour yourself over me, Holy Spirit.

I'm learning about living, about
being alive.
Today, I trust you. And tomorrow,
I will trust you.
At every moment, I will trust in
your completed works.

I will trust you are doing your
will, even (especially) when I
don't understand. I don't do well
outside of you.

Disciple me, as I admit my
dependence on you.
May I become an expert in the
art of following.

Fretting

December 2012

Sometimes, I feel like a car speeding along faster than my feeble engine can handle. I pray hard partly from love, but partly from fear. I worry if God doesn't hold me together, my wheels might spin off.

I flew back to Hong Kong recently, and now I'm more confused than ever where I should be. Hong Kong is home; I want to be with my dad, I want to comfort my mum and I want to have her incredible homemade soups twice a week (Chinatown offerings just don't come close). New York is . . . I don't know. I'm learning the hard way about labor restrictions against my visa status: a month ago I was asked to leave in the middle of rehearsing a union-regulated production that apparently my VISA restricted me from. I love singing, but I'm questioning whether other people love it when I sing. Frankly, I feel like the city is retracting her once welcoming arms and awkwardly darting her eyes away me.

Yet, when I look into the mirror, I see New York. And I can't shake a guttural sense that God has led me here for . . . something.

I wish I knew what that something was. I'm working so hard to feel purposeful, but my striving isn't quieting the doubts reverberating through my system.

I want to stop my car and take a breath, but I haven't used the brakes in so long I don't even know where they are anymore.

December 9

Lord, I often feel paralyzed.

I suppose it's no wonder — I have such a terrible habit of taking my eyes off of you. It's funny how I can see the problem, and even the solution, but I just stay paralyzed.

Well. It's not funny at all.

December 12

Lord, I've been so restless! So aimless and yet so desperate for something. I don't know what it is. I'm not at peace with where I am, and my heart is noisy.

Lord, I confess I'm desperate for my career to blossom. I've been letting that take up all my mind space, and I really don't like that. I don't want that to be me.

Every day, let me die and rise with you — a daily baptism. Let me be one with you in spirit.
I need your peace, God.
I need your clarity.

Don't let me be desperate for anything but you.
I don't want to be that woman who will go anywhere and do anything to find instant satisfaction.[1] I don't need that. I don't want that. I won't be fooled.

I want you.

December 14

RESTLESS.
RESTLESS.
RESTLESS.
RESTLESS.
RESTLESS.
RESTLESS.
AHHHHHHH.
RESTLESS.
RESTLESS.
RESTLESS.

I'm itching to do something great. I know that's obnoxious.
But it's where I am right at this moment.
BAHHHHH.

Music.
Why do I make music?
Because I think it moves people like nothing else.
Words are power.
Words with a melody is power multiplied.
There's a reason angels sing.
I believe in singing.
I believe in pouring my voice out into open spaces.
Lord, even you move to music.[1]
You respond to cymbals and lyres.

But man is born to trouble
as the sparks fly upward.

Job 5:7

BORN TO TROUBLE.
Sometimes I wonder:
What exactly am I made of?
Was I born to trouble? Depths
of trouble?

I feel like a flying fish sometimes.
I'm the awkward flapping fish.

Christ, you are my wings.
You make me supernatural.
With you, I can soar.
We rise from the ocean up.

December 22

I think songwriting is about listening.
    Listening to what my soul is singing.
    What angels are singing, proclaiming.
    What your spirit is singing, proclaiming.
I want to be in tune with that.

Lord, I want nothing more right now than to live in your sound. What do you sound like?

December 28

I watched a really good movie today.
I kept thinking, I WANT TO CREATE BEAUTIFUL THINGS
SO BADLY!
And I wondered, Where does that desire come from? Do I
need to suppress it?

I decided no.

Those desires don't need suppression. They need
submission. To be committed to you, as I trust with all my
heart that you are making my path straight.

Commit your way to the Lord;
trust in him, and he will act.

Psalm 37:5

What is my way?
My life? My dreams? My methods?
Okay! They're yours, Lord! I commit them to you! (I think!)
I am yours, and you are mine.[1]

I will not subscribe to the ways of this world and its narrow
definition of beauty.
I desire the beauty of your design.

January 14

Back in the city.
Funny. I think this is the first time I'm feeling like I'm coming home rather "going back to New York."

I do, Lord.
I do feel you calling me to be here.

I will give you every place where you set your foot . . .

Joshua 1:3 (NIV)

Will you really give me every place my foot treads upon?

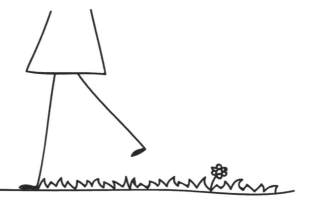

January 15

Today I want to worship you in a new way.
I want to be closer to you than I was yesterday.
I want to write you a love letter every day, because you are my first love. The first one who taught me about love.

I belong to you.

Please God, help me to stop being afraid of other people's words and thoughts. I only want to fear you.

February 19

You know what I realized?
I know shame better than I
know acceptance.
I know shame so well.
I live in it a lot.

Could I put a stop to that?

How does the beloved relate to the lover?
    With joy
    With delight
    With hope
    With confidence of a response
    With peace
    With anticipation
    With no fear

Thank you, Father.

February 20

Father, I trust your will.

Take the songs I write, and use them however you desire. They're your songs anyway, because I'm yours. Guide me as I move forward.

My greatest desire and joy is your will being done. I love your perfect will! I can trust your plan completely. Where you lead me, I can gladly go, because you are with me, and you are my strength.

God, it's true what you say: apart from you, I can do nothing.[1] Nothing of value. Nothing that fulfills me.

Father, I return to your peace. The peace of your good and perfect will.

that's you, Lord, my strength!

February 21

I'm sitting in the studio,
working on a song.
Lord, I love you.
Jesus, I sing in your name.
I pray my work will sow seeds and
give life.

March 10

When I read about that woman in Luke this morning, washing your feet with her tears and her hair,[1] I saw myself in her. Or I wanted to.

I want to be at your feet, Jesus, so badly.

I need to be near you, so the world can fade away. I want to see what you see, wipe my tears, sit next to you and lean on your chest like your disciple did.[2]

March 12

Now faith is confidence in what we hope for and assurance about what we do not see.

Hebrews 11:1 (NIV)

Lord, I hope for you, though I don't see you.
I want to live by the substance of faith.
I want to be comfortable with not seeing.
Is that possible, God?
Can I be that close to you?

hello?

Father, draw me into your throne room, and then let me stay there.

March 14

Martha, Martha, the Lord answered.

Luke 10:41 (NIV)

Mara, Mara.

I worry and fret about so many things!
Most things.
What am I not believing?
Do I not think my God will provide?
Do I not know who I am?
Am I so forgetful?

Mary chose that one thing.[1]

Only you, Lord.
I worship you.
I adore you.

March 26

Father, you have brought me here. Please show me how you would like me to move forward. Your will be done at every point in my journey. I want to be brave through obedience, not through blindness. I want to be recklessly dependent, not stubbornly independent.

You place me on a mountaintop, where it is easier to dream with you.

I pray my songs are like a tree, bearing much fruit.[1] Providing shade. That birds will come to rest. I pray everyone who waters this tree will be blessed tenfold. This tree is planted by your streams. It's a part of the landscape of your love. It completes the picture of your kingdom.

April 1

God, we are speaking to each other.

Thank you for giving your son that I might have the
boldness to say things like that.

You make me beautiful.
I want to be as beautiful as you!

As I was walking down the street today, I actually felt my
spirit leap with joy — like my soul is content because I am
truly walking the path I am called to. I want to remember
that. I want to remember this certainty, in this moment —
that God is with me. He has brought me here.

And we can dance here. We can be glad together here.
Father, thank you, thank you.

You chose me.
You're right here in this room
with me.
I love you!

April 14

I'm scared right now.
I'm scared of not knowing what I'm doing. Scared of going for the wrong things. Scared I'm all wrong.

<u>Do not fear</u>

I'm trying

Restore me, oh God.

April 17

Father, how do you want me to dream?
What do you dream for me?
I know you've put music in my heart.
And I see you move in my work.
Help me to know what to do with these desires in my life!

Commit your work to the Lord,
and your plans will be established.

Proverbs 16:3

I am trusting you to guide the direction of my work.
I will not measure success by money — but by your delight.
In fact, I will take joy in knowing I am already successful,
because I'm living according to desires you placed in me.

Lord, stop me if I go the wrong way. I'd rather have the
world as I know it crash around me than go the way
against your pleasure. Your pleasure is my joy.

April 27

Shall I bring to the point of birth and not cause to bring forth? says the Lord;
Shall I, who cause to bring forth, shut the womb? says your God.

Isaiah 66:9

I brought you to the point of birth.
Shall I not cause to bring forth?
Says my God.

I'm putting away my fears now.
Thank you.

May 20

Dear sweet, heavenly Father.

You hold my life, my world in your hand,[1] and that's the way I want it. I worship you and no other. Thank you, Father, for being accessible to me through Jesus Christ.[2] I love being able to write to you. And I pray the distance between us, in whatever sense, only ever decreases. You are a holy God. Completely Holy. Perfect in every way beyond my comprehension. Your plans are good and your gifts are perfect. I trust that you are leading me. I trust your guidance and your ever-presence.

Thank you for loving me.
Thank you for calling me.

Lord, forgive me when I am seduced by the lures of this world. Forgive me when I let other things and other people satisfy what is my hunger for you. Forgive me for not living on your word, for not loving my neighbor as myself. Forgive me when I allow lustful thoughts into the temple of my body. I have not been zealous for my Father's glory — at least not as King David and Jesus before me were.

Lord! I want to be! I want to be consumed by passion for
your holy name.
Forgive my unfaithfulness. I've been the flower tossed by
the waves. I would like to turn this page.

Let my life sing your name.
Like King David.
I want to live in your love.
Inside it.
I want to make a home inside your love.

Your love

June 15

Sweet, sweet Lord,
Oh, that my ways may be steadfast
in keeping your statutes!
That I cannot help but honor you with my whole being.
That my life screams your name and your great grace.
I have stored up your word in my heart,
Tucked inside, so deep inside it can't be removed.
I will delight in your statutes;
They will be my joy.
I will know them more, and rejoice in them even more.
I will run in the way of your commandments
when you enlarge my heart!
Until my heart is nearly as big as yours!
Make your commands, your will and your ways the melody
of my life!

Psalm 119: 5, 11, 16, 32

July 7

Father, I am so anxious to do great things again. I'm almost struggling to focus because I just want great things to happen.
Then I get frustrated, and maybe a little mad.
This must be a repetitive cycle for you to watch . . .

Lord, I don't want to be blinded by my ideas, my vision.
My life is yours. Yours to take, break, bless and give.
I submit my will and my desires to you, because my soul knows that you alone can satisfy my every longing.
Success and failure within my work means nothing outside of you. I don't even want to be successful according to this world's definition if I am not first delighting myself in you!
Father? Your will be done — as it pleases you.

I want to watch you do great things. And I want to be smiling at you while your glory shines all around.
Forgive me my impatience and my regular silliness.
May your grace abound in my bumbling efforts.
And may I serve you in those bumbling efforts.
May you take delight in my perseverance.
Father, guide me forward.

The Lord will fight for you; you need only to be still.

Exodus 14:14

I need only to be still.

July 20

Lord, I come to you now.
To be with you.
To present my heart.

Examine my heart, Lord.[1]
What do you see?

July 21

Father, I feel my need of you today.
Come to my rescue.
I am in need of your power and your deliverance.
Because you are stronger than me.

You broke sin.

Father come and rule in me —
Rule in my heart.
I am yearning for you!
I am longing for your touch.
Longing to hear your voice here.

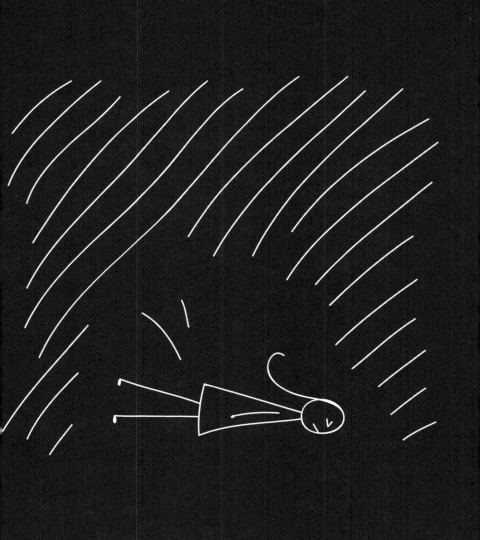

July 2013

When I first struggled to get out of bed at the beginning of the month, I was confused. I am a pronounced morning person, so lethargy was new to me. I didn't think much of it, though. Maybe the summer heat?

Within a week, every other part of my day likewise was becoming a struggle. I found myself crying for little reason hours at a time. I started canceling appointments. One day I just lay on the ground, unable to get up.

I Googled PMS to see if I was dealing with some lady troubles. The symptoms matched: anxiety, depressed mood, crying spells, appetite changes, social withdrawal, poor concentration, headache, fatigue . . . I was almost relieved when I realized I was experiencing no more than a monthly hump — just a bad case of *PMS*.

But when the bad days persisted and grew in intensity, I was back at my computer, this time typing in *Symptoms of Depression*.

Loss of energy almost every day? Yes.

Feelings of guilt or worthlessness? Yes.

Impaired concentration? Yes.

Insomnia or hypersomnia? Yes.

Markedly diminished interest in most activities? Yes.

Feeling slowed down? Yes.

Recurring thoughts of death? Unfortunately, yes.

It was like waking into a slow-motion nightmare. I never knew I had this darkness lurking inside. The dead weight of despair now clings to me like flies to a rotting apple and I can hardly remember a time when my smiles weren't forced. When I look in the mirror, I see a tired body and a weeping soul.

I am stuck, wheels in a swamp. And I am calling for help.

July 23

I don't know what is happening.

Lord, I'm feeling incredibly fragile.
I feel like I don't know how to go on.
Please help me.
Help me to seek help.

I feel like I might break at any moment.
Except that I know you hold me together.
And you are a mighty glue.
You keep my pieces together.

When I am weak, you are strong.[1]
Though I am blind, you can see.
When I am afraid, you are there.

July 24

Lord I need you.
I need you. I need you.
With every breath I need you.
You are my hope.
You are my rock.
You are my helper.
You are my defender.
You are my joy.

I don't feel like I have a purpose.
I feel worthless.
I can't find joy.
Everything seems totally meaningless.[1]
I'm tired of myself.
I don't know what I'm doing.
I'm hurting.

Help me, help me, please.
I'm so desperate for you.
I need to feel your presence.
I want to be healed in your presence.
Speak to me as I sleep.
Help me to love myself.

August 8

Can't sleep.

Lord, what is weighing me down?
What is keeping me from being free?
I'm not living in freedom right now. I feel bondage. I feel like I've been shot in the foot and I've been dragging it forward. Holy Spirit — show me what is going on! What is happening? Why am I not free?

Why am I downcast?
Am I not receiving your love?
Am I not believing the things you say about me?
Why did you create me?
Why am I alive?
My soul is heavy.

You say:
Come to me, all ye who are weary
and heavy laden,
and I will give you rest.[1]
I need your rest, Lord.
I need your peace.
I need your blessing.
I have no focus now. No direction.
I'm lost.

LORD. DO SOMETHING.

I feel silly saying that, but I mean it. Don't let me go on like
this.
I need something from you.
No, I need you.
I need you.
Feed me, help me, nurse me.
I feel sorry for being so weak, so selfish, so self-focused.

But I don't know what else to do because I'm not okay
now.
I feel like such a broken record!
The most broken record there ever was.
I am tired of my thoughts.
There is nothing new under my sun.[2]
Please be my sun.
Take me somewhere.
Please.
I can't go anywhere on my own right now. I can't move.
I need you to take me.
I am crying out to you, Lord.
Listen to my pen.
I am desperate for your restoration.
Not just for me, Lord; I want to become a spring so I can
water the desert around me.[3]
I am no different from the desert now.
I am as dry as roasted seaweed.

DO SOMETHING, LORD.
Forgive me if I am praying a stupid prayer.
Forgive me anyway because I sin against you too much.
I hurt you too much.
I don't want to. I want to live.
I want your Holy Spirit to make me beautiful.

Help me, Lord.
Help me.
Answer me.[4]
I am surrounded by clouds and heavy fog.
I feel weak and needy.
Wake me.
Shake me.
Help. Help. Help.
I'm not going to anyone or anything else.
I'm not turning to idols to fix me.

I'm turning to you.
I'm turning to the almighty God.

CAN YOU HEAR ME?
You alone can be my refuge.
You alone can understand my cry.
You alone are beautiful.
You alone can answer me in my deep distress.
I am in distress, Lord.
WHERE ARE YOU?

Naked Prayers

I'm sorry.
I'm yours, Lord.
Don't let me feel so alone and dark.
Don't let me stay here.
It's been too long already.
Forgive me my pride.
My stubbornness.
I know I need you every hour.
I am like a fish on land.
I can't do anything.
I don't see what you see.
I just see my tail and it looks so silly.
Where are you now?
Jesus, had you been here?
Do you know this place?

I am tired.
Heal me. Help me.
Call to me, Abba.
Let me hear your love for me.

August 9

I am still empty, Lord. Still waiting for you. I feel more and more removed, and I'm trying harder and harder not to be.

Conversations are such an effort. But I'm trying to keep having them because they seem important to keep having.

Lord, don't be far from me.[1]
You are far from me now.
I can't see you, and I don't know what your thoughts are toward me.

Where are you?? Why can't I feel anything? Or, do I feel too much?

I know this will pass. I do. And I praise you, God.
But meanwhile, I'm so hollow, so hollow . . .
Help me stand.
Even lying down is tiring.
Help me be free.
I don't think I have any sight now.
What do you want me to do now?

How . . .

My soul is tired.
But I hold on to hope.

I hold on to restoration.
I know that's what you do.
I know you are providing for me right now.
Help me receive.
Help me love.
Help me live . . .

I feel like something's been taken from me.
Don't know where to get it back.
Something's missing, but at least I believe that I'm made to
be full.

Help me not to feel so alone.
Help me to trust what I need to trust.
I'm empty now. Again again again.
Lord, it hurts when I don't feel you.

August 12

Father?
I am here.
I am yours.
I am surrendered to you.
I love you. I want you.
What are you saying?

ECHO

ECHO

ECHO

ECHO

August 13

Father.
You are big and beautiful.
I am small and beautiful.
My future — yours, truly.
I'm living one day at a time, Lord.
One day at a time.
I know you are mine.

Show me the way forward when you declare the time is right.
I trust in your timing.

August 17

Birthday. I only want to cry now.

I think sometimes I hurt because I don't know
how to tell people what I need. And I need
so much. It's frightening. And I see people's
needs. So much need everywhere. And I can't
meet any of them . . .

Lord, I need you to restore me this coming year.
I need your healing. I need your nearness.

Help me to live for you and your sheep. Help me to
lay everything down.
Give me joy, Lord, give me joy.
Draw close to me, my Lord.
Thank you for waking me up today.
I love you.
I love you so much.
Be ever near to me, Lord.

August 21

Lord, often I realize I have no idea what to pray for. I have no idea how your vision can become mine, how things would look were I wholly surrendered to you . . . but I want to come close to that.

Father, I think sometimes I'm like a car trying to move forward with a steep mountain in front of me. And I'm just driving into it over and over again, not admitting that I just don't have the power to move mountains.

I need your help, God. No more relying on my own run-down car.

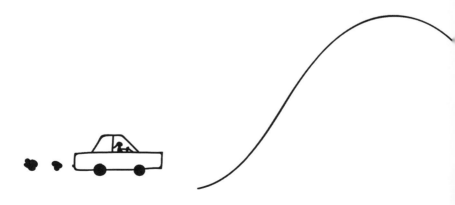

August 26

BAM
BAM
BAM

That's me feeling crushed.

Lord, lift this spirit of depression. Lift it and take it far from me. I am closer to you than I am to darkness. You reign in my life. Nothing else. I wholly belong to you. You hold me together by your spirit.

Help me let go.
Let go of my expectations, my fears.
I pray I can dance before you again.
I want to be free, Jesus.
You came to free me.[1]

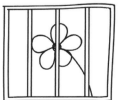

August 31

Good morning, dear Lord.
I come before you today with a renewed mind.
I long to meet you and experience you in a new way.
I know I need the empowerment of the Holy Spirit.
I need to know that you are with me.
As you were with Abraham.
Revive me!
I am drowning.
But I believe you will lift me up, you will hold me to you, and when you place me back on the waters, I will stand.

Falling

September 1

God, I sit before you this morning.
I want to get up later with a greater sense of your nearness.
Draw near to me, Lord, as I draw near to you.[1]

Father, I know there's a wound in me.
I know there is an open wound that's been causing pain,
and I want to be healed.
I believe you are a God who heals.
Reveal things to me. Show me your thoughts.
Give me strength to continue this journey.

When you pass through the waters,
I will be with you;
When you pass through the rivers,
they will not sweep over you.
When you walk through the fire,
You will not be burned;
The flames will not set you ablaze.

Isaiah 43:2 (NIV)

Lord, I struggle to believe that you are really with me.

Never will I leave you;
never will I forsake you.

Hebrews 13:5 (NIV)

Okay.
Father, I know you are greater than my feelings. I know
there is a world outside my feelings. Spirit, free me from
this glass trap.
Free me!
Jesus, teach me to walk like you did. I want to be
completely like you.
Take my lips, Lord.
Make them totally yours.
Let them only speak the truth.

September 2

Thank you for this day, Father.
Today, I remember that nothing is impossible through Christ
who strengthens me.[1]
May that promise dwell richly in me.

Lord, you give me all that I need.
Help me to remember that!

Thank you, Lord:
    For your power
    For your work in every Christian
    For encouraging me
    For showing up here
    For your presence
    For your strength
    For your people
    For the ways you have worked in our lives
    For loving me
    For calling me
    For my voice

I'm on my way home now, and the weight of sadness and
loneliness is coming back.
I feel lonely again.
Lord, I know you are still here.
I want to let you fill me.

Falling

Be my joy, Lord.
Protect me.
Protect me from the schemes of the evil one.
Let the shield of faith protect me from all the arrows.[2]
You never leave me or forsake me.
I'm so sad again, Lord!
Do I need to know why this is happening?

When evil comes against me, I will resist the devil and he
will flee.[3]
I will reject the enemy's lies.
I belong to Jesus.
I know that I am loved.
I believe that I am yours.
And that you are mighty to save.
I believe you want to make me whole.
Your word is my life. My light.
I will seek you and I will find you.[4]

helmet of salvation

sword of
the spirit

shield of faith

breastplate of
righteousness

belt of truth

gospel of peace

September 3

Thank you for waking me. Thank you for sustaining me.
In you there is no darkness.[1]
Lord, I love you and I need you.
I need you every hour.
You are my hope for today.
Father, in your mercy, in your grace, lift this depression.
Deliver me and place me on a rock.
Help me to restore my vision, and let me see things as they
are.
I need you to help me.
Thank you.
I'm going to walk this day in light.

*We rejoice in our sufferings, knowing that suffering
produces endurance, and endurance produces character,
and character produces hope, and hope does not put us
to shame, because God's love has been poured into our
hearts through the Holy Spirit who has been given to us.*

Romans 5:3-5

Hope does not disappoint.

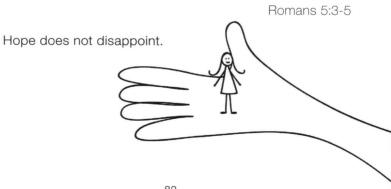

September 4

I am very anxious today.
But I come to you first.
You are great and awesome, Lord.
Your name be lifted high above every other name.

Father, let your will be done in my life today. Let your word
dwell richly in me. I will stay close to you today. As I go now
to do my work, come with me. Join me, as I join you.

I pray your presence follows me.
Thank you, dear, dear Lord.

September 5

Yesterday was a very difficult day.
A lot of pain, a lot of tears.
But as I prayed I saw an image of a house with six
windows, and I saw that one of the windows had opened. I
felt like I was the house and light is entering slowly.

Lord? Help me to pray to you as you like to be prayed to.
That's what I want.

Jesus, I ask for healing.
I know you hear.
And I await your total deliverance.

Falling

September 6

Lord, I'm exhausted all the time.
I struggle to move.
My head is very heavy.
I can't remember anything.

Uphold me, Lord.
Be near me.
I need —

I need.

September 7

Thank you for being my portion.[1]
I didn't know what portion meant.
But I think I'm seeing now.
Somehow, you are my portion — what I need for today.

As I sleep, let your angels minister to me. I pray I wake up
with strength and hope.

Tonight, I looked in the mirror. I cried, and I prayed:
Make this beautiful.

September 8

Still in darkness.
Depression feels like drowning in oatmeal.
Bland. Dark. Repetitive. Moist.

Oh God, I need you.
I need your spirit to fill me.
To breathe life into these parched bones.
My bones are cracked and dry.[1]
It hurts to move.
My energy is like water stored in a broken jar, draining out
faster than I can refill.
Mend this broken jar!

September 9

Psalm 91 says,

He who dwells in the shelter of the Most High
will abide in the shadow of the Almighty.
I will say to the Lord, My refuge and my fortress,
my God, in whom I trust.
For he will deliver you from the snare of the fowler
and from the deadly pestilence.
He will cover you with his pinions,
and under his wings you will find refuge;
his faithfulness is a shield and buckler.
You will not fear the terror of the night,
nor the arrow that flies by day,
nor the pestilence that stalks in darkness,
nor the destruction that wastes at noonday.

So I will not be afraid.

September 13

I want you to piece me together — again.
I want to be functional again.
I don't want to stay like this, Lord.
This is not the way I want to spend my life.
But I trust you.
I do.

I like you, Lord.

September 15

Let go

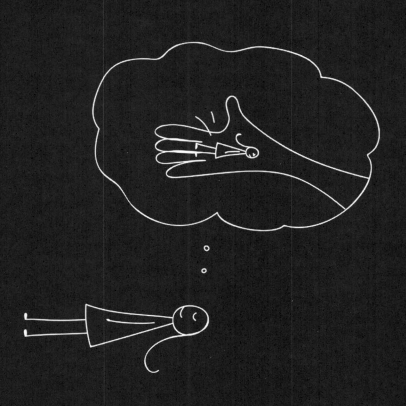

Finding

September 2013

I didn't want help from anyone at the beginning.

When my boyfriend, Mark, suggested counseling, I said no. I wanted God to wave a magic wand and miraculously make me better, which would be the only clear evidence that He had heard my prayers. If He really loves me, and He can do anything, why wouldn't He just heal me? Had I done something horribly wrong? Did God turn away from me? The questions tirelessly danced around me.

I guess Mark did not take no for an answer. My phone rang one afternoon when I was having a particularly torturous few hours, and before the lady could get through her introduction and explain how she got my number, I was sobbing and crying for help. I told her I was scared, that I didn't know what was happening to me, that everything was getting too difficult. We set up an appointment.

I felt like I had lost. I always thought I was a healthy person, a strong Christian. I guess I imagined that last label had meant I would be, well, a bit of a superhuman. I knew that my father's failing health had been difficult for my whole family, but doesn't trusting in God mean He can put my pain in a box and make it disappear? I knew I'd been overworking myself, but doesn't trusting in God mean He can give me the ability to push past my body's limits? I can do all things through Him, right? RIGHT?

Within thirty minutes of my first conversation with a very gentle counselor, my eyes opened to a truckload of misconceptions I had been driving around. I started seeing how my wrong thinking had been a slow poison to my mind. No, I am not invincible. Yes, you can know God's love and still struggle with mood disorders. No, my worth is not dependent on my mental health. Yes, God is loving me even when I'm miserable. And, well, I may never know why He didn't wave my pain away. Do I need to?

I am beginning to let go. I surrender my perception of strength, my idea of success, and my feeble attempts to save myself. And as I release the dead weight of once poisonous beliefs, my reflection is slowly stirring to life.

All of this is exhausting, but liberating.

September 17

Lord, forgive me.
I see more clearly now. For a very long time, I made an idol
of productivity and labor. Rather than basing my worth on
you, I based my worth on the meager work of my hands.
Forgive me, Lord.

My worth is not dependent on my work.[1]
My worth is great because of Jesus.

I love you, Lord.
Holy one, make me like you.

September 18

Thank you, Lord, for this journey.
It's exhausting but I'm glad we are walking together, and I know that you cannot, will not, do not want to abandon me. You are with me. I am not alone.

I see a light at this tunnel's end; I see my restoration and I await the day I stand in freedom and praise you with a full heart.

Lord, I love you, and I love your people who are loving me on your behalf.

September 20

I'm exhausted.
Thoroughly tired.
My body is tense as a bullet and my brain is firing blanks in every direction.

Lord?
Teach me to live?

September 22

I'm so anxious I feel as though I'm about to explode. My heart feels like it's expanding out of my chest and something terrible is about to happen.

But what I know is that, Jesus, you are king of the storm.

You calm the raging seas.[1]
You hold my gaze as you give me your peace — not the peace that the world gives but a greater one that can carry me through the storm.

Lord, I will not worry!
I will NOT be anxious.
Because you are stronger.
And you have saved me.
You have lifted me above my enemies.
I trust in you.

<u>I am on the boat with you</u>

September 25

Father, in my absolute emotional fragility, you are my rock, on whom I do not falter.

As I struggle to get through this day, I remember that you do not struggle to take care of me.

While my desire to live is weak, your desire for me to live is glorious.

Don't be deceived, my dear brothers and sisters. Every good and perfect gift is from above, coming down from the Father of the heavenly lights, who does not change like shifting shadows.

James 1:16-17 (NIV)

How great you are
>for your unchanging nature,
>for your unfailing love for me,
>for your constant goodness toward me.
>Everything good I have comes from you.[1]

He chose to give us birth . . .

James 1:18 (NIV)

I am your choice, along with those around me. There is SO

much I do not comprehend, Lord, but your love — I know in
my soul — it is real, and mightily powerful.

September 27

Lord?

Sometimes I wonder, is this what it means to be an adult?
This heaviness I have to carry around?

But no, you invite us to be reborn, to be a child again.[1]
This is not what it is to be a child. I'm playing the part of a
tortured soul.

Right now, you are with me and your love abounds.
Lord, help me to reject all that is not from you.
Help me to see you, see myself, and see your people for
what we really are.

So if the Son sets you free, you will be free indeed.

John 8:36

Freedom is a hope and not a reality in my life right now.
Bring me to where freedom is the reality, Lord.

How long till I am whole again?
I long for wholeness.
I long to be complete — I in you, you in me.
My soul is weary, so I come to you. Give me rest, Lord.

September 28

Consider it pure joy, my brothers and sisters, whenever you face trials of many kinds, because you know that the testing of your faith produces perseverance. Let perseverance finish its work so that you may be mature and complete, not lacking anything.

James 1:2-4 (NIV)

Pure joy . . . Bah.

Okay, Lord, my hope:
That when perseverance finishes its work, I will be mature and complete, not lacking anything.
I'm going to believe that is possible.

Yes Father, though the winds are raging and howling — yet I will fix my eyes on Jesus, the one who understands. I will look at His finished work on the cross. I will call on His name, which saves.
Jesus, complete me just as you were made complete.
All that is ahead, I surrender to you.

Bless this day, my Father, give me strength to move. Give me joy to breathe. Help me to stand on your truth through this roller coaster.

September 29

Oh God.
Help. Help. Help. Help.
My soul is dying.
Or so it feels.

God — I don't want to feel anymore.
And yet I do.
   I want to feel your love.
   I want to feel your closeness.
   I want to feel your touch.

Make me whole!
Make me whole!
Wholly yours.
I want to live my days with purpose.

Help me!
I am sick with anguish.
Lord, I need you.
Today my head is too much for my body.

September 30

Good morning, Lord.
I feel warmer today.
Thank you.

Prepare my heart, mind and body for what you have for me.
And I will receive.

*But the wisdom from above is first pure, then peaceable,
gentle, open to reason, full of mercy and good fruits,
impartial and sincere.*

James 3:17

Yes, that's the wisdom I need!

October 1

I realized yesterday — no matter what I say, I do long for riches and fame, and I subconsciously live in anticipation of both. No wonder I feel a deep sense of frustration as long as I don't have them.

God, teach me once again the meaning of success. Teach me its definition in the context of your love and your truth and your grace.

Grace.

Thank you Jesus, for dying for me while I was yet a sinner.
When you look at me, you see your child — thank you.
I will live in that title: Child.
I let go of chasing other things, Father.

Forgive me, Lord.
You are my first. The first love of
my soul. I love you, dear Father.

I praise you for I am fearfully and wonderfully made!

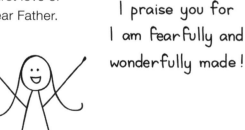

October 2

Be patient and stand firm.

James 5:8 (NIV)

Okay, God.

Father, I pray I seek you in the way you want to be sought. Early in the morning I will come to you and ask, what are you doing? How can I be in your story today? What do I need to deny, Lord?

Today —
What is keeping me from following you with my whole self?

FEAR.
Fear of others. Fear of uncertainty. Fear of humiliation. Fear of being wrong.

SELF-DOUBT.
Looking to myself more than I look to you.

Lord, my fears and doubts I give to you.
Take them and throw them far away from me as I fill my mind with your truth.

I love you, Lord, so much.
I can't wait to be with you.

October 4

The prayer of a righteous person has great power as it is working.

James 5:16

Jesus, today I receive your righteousness.
Thank you for extending it to me.
I'm at your throne now; thank you for welcoming me.

Father . . . sometimes, I'm very embarrassed to say, I don't think I believe that you love me more than I love you. I'm sorry!

But your love bends trees.

October 5

I need you today.
Like I did yesterday.
Like I did the day before.

I adore you.
I live in you. Remain in you.
Lord, hold me all day, every day.

October 6

Let your light shine before others, so that they may see your good works and give glory to your Father who is in heaven.

Matthew 5:16

What is my light?
Your story. The evidence of your work in my mess.

Lord, I know I am helpless before you.
I have no way to help myself, and I don't know how to help anyone around me.
But you are willing and able; I know that.
So be our help.

I feel naked and vulnerable.
I need your comfort and your encouragement.
I will wait for you in the stillness.
You delight in our secret meetings.

October 7

Father, I have so much to learn.
I live in constant fear, though I know I don't have to.
I fear people, danger, pain, evil, myself and my foolishness.
Lord, your perfect love drives out fear.[1]
Drive out the fear in me and leave only the fear of you.
Father, I pray that I find my personality in you, before you.
Help me to shine like a courageous star.
Thank you for listening.
In Jesus' name.

[Several hours later]

The heaviness hit me an hour ago, now my head is hurting.
Lord — come to me now —
Come to me and breathe.

I am not alone.
I am not alone.
God . . . I hate what is my life right now.

I feel rage about my uselessness.

I hate this.
Save me.

October 8

You say, I am no longer your servant, but your child.
I am your son, with whom you are well pleased.
You are the vine.
I am the branches.

I speak.

You speak.

I am wasting time.

I am working in you.[1]

I am useless.

*You are bought with
an incredible price because of
my great love for you.[2]*

I am so selfish.

*Everyone is selfish until
they live by the spirit —
I knew that from the beginning.[3]*

Form my soul in you, Lord. Yes, I believe that, in my
suffering, you are forming things in me. Creating glory in
me.

the leaves are
growing again

October 9

Heavenly Father:
Help me!
I've been calling to you.
Please come to me.
I really need you.
I need you to come near to me.
Help.
Help.
Help.
Help.
Help.

Regardless, I will love you, Lord, my strength; I will hold
on to you.
If I live the rest of my life like this, I will still hold on to you.
You are my portion, my daily bread.
I will trust in your unfailing love.
I can't wait to see you, Lord!

It's okay. Purify me. I hate the process, but I love you.
I love you more than I love being happy.

October 10

Good morning, Father.
How are you?
I'm better.
I'm thankful there's no pain today.

Move through my voice tonight.
Stir people's hearts through our songs, I pray.
Make me a channel of your peace![1]

October 11

Thank you.
Jesus, you are stunning.
May my heart be stunning, like you.

The desire of the righteous ends only in good.

Proverbs 11:23

I desire your presence.
I desire to see your glory fill the earth, so that every corner
glows with your light.
I desire a life of close fellowship with you.
I desire a mind that is always renewed by your nearness.
May these desires end in good.

October 12

Oh lover,
my heart
said she knew you well,
but when I asked her your name
she couldn't tell
and made her silence swell
against my chest
until I had to cough,
excuse me.

October 13

Lord, give me wisdom.
Your light is my guide.
Who am I to make plans and say what will come
tomorrow?[1]
It's you I'm living for.
You, who gave me a heart and a voice.
You, the rock of my hope.

I love you.
I am with you.
Fill me completely so I can fill the world with you!

October 18

God?
I'm not just paying you lip service; I want to honor you with my whole life.
I want to be pleasing to you.
I know my flesh is weak, full of wicked desires, driven by self-fulfilment, but I want to honor you more than I honor my own fickle will.

When I am being foolish, open my eyes.
When I am being unfaithful, shine your light.

When I am walking away from you, touch my feet.
I give you access to all of me.

October 26

My God, my God.
Your name, Your presence fills my mind with beauty.
I am in love with you.

Take me deeper into your truth.
Draw me into you, Lord.
Hem me in, behind and before,[1] until your breath is
upon me.
You breathe life into me, and I can do nothing apart
from you.
Lord, I want to be held by you.
I want to know your arms.
Bring me close.

rain on me

October 27

Lord!

You are my source!
Make my heart beat for you!
Make my lips sing your story!
You are worthy to be adored, worthy to be gazed upon,
every hour of my days.

Help me to live by the spirit, walk by the spirit, be led by the
spirit, that I may have life, and life to the fullest.[1]
You bring me great joy!
You cause my heart to desire:
I desire growing intimacy with the only one who knows me
completely.

October 29

Lord, I am a bit sad today.
But I love you with all my ability.
And lack of ability.

November 12

Good morning, Father.
Thank you for waking me up today.

I know now:
I need you every hour.

Every hour, I need you.

November 14

Father, thank you for healing me. So slowly, but so surely. I can almost taste the freedom you give.

Afterword

November 14, 2013 is the last entry in this book, but it was by no means the end of this journey. I thought I was better, and then I wasn't; then I was, then I wasn't. A part of me badly wants to tie up my story in a cute little polka dot bow — but that would be a lie.

In reality, I struggled for several more months before I finally reached a place of relative stability. I end this book here because my story took a turn after this point and in a few more months I found myself engaged to the most wonderful man who saw me through my absolute worst. Mark became an integral part of the next chapter in my story, and we walked what followed hand in hand.

In the midst of my struggle, I had wondered why God wouldn't just snap His fingers and lift depression far, far away from me the first time I prayed for help. Why did He let me cry for hours, days, weeks, then months? Why did He let me suffer?

I still don't have the perfect answer, but I have some thoughts.

I hated every second of what I went through, and a part of me is terrified of falling into that darkness once again. But another part of me knows that if I had not fallen, I would not have realized that I had been walking with a limp for a very long time. Before depression, I thought there was nothing wrong with me. I was the hopeful college grad, eager to make a positive impact in this world. I never imagined I would find myself struggling to get out of bed and crying on the bathroom floor on my birthday. Yet when I look back now, I see that I had been broken long before the period covered in this book — I just didn't know it.

When you only ever look in the mirror with your best outfit, you forget the bruises and scars beneath: the low self-esteem, the confused identity and the lie that you are only as good as your work. When I think back, the year I spent in Ethiopia had been a luxury. The simple lifestyle made it easy to strip naked in my time with God. Living in a cutthroat city like New York though, I pile on the layers to puff myself up until I am almost invincible. I shun vulnerability, pretend I'm fine — and pay the consequence.

Would it be more loving if God had waved a magic wand and made me happy that first day I cried to Him? Would He be a better Father if He had swept all my underlying fears and insecurities under the carpet?

I wish. But I don't think so.

I hate pain. I suspect God does, too. But if I hadn't fallen, if God had been "loving" and kept me rolled up in layers of bubble wrap, I would not have known that I never dealt with the grief that came with my father's failing health, that I have a terrible habit of numbing my pain through my work, and that, well, I have a bizarre notion that believing in God makes me a superman.

I still struggle. Watching my father suffer will never get

easier. I have a better relationship with my work, but you can bet there are still days I am convinced my world would be a better place if I could just record an earth-shatteringly awesome album.

But maybe the one lesson that was (thankfully) forced upon me is that truly, I am no superman. *Following* God is not *being* God. He created me with my strengths and weaknesses and He loves me for them. Superman's narrative is not my story; that's for the comics. My life is a much more wonderfully messy jumble of highs and lows.

The meaning of prayer to me is constantly evolving. At the beginning of this book, I mentioned that I see prayer as a girl looking into a mirror. I think that image has expanded for me. These days, I see prayer as a whole gathering of people looking into the mirror, and I'm only one of them. And this mirror doesn't just reflect what the naked eye can see. When I look into this mirror, I see more than what I am now. I see what I was made to be.

I see what we are now, and what we are made to be.

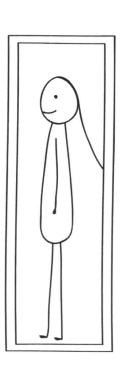

October 19

¹Matthew 3:1-4

In those days John the Baptist came preaching in the wilderness of Judea, "Repent, for the kingdom of heaven is at hand." For this is he who was spoken of by the prophet Isaiah when he said,
"The voice of one crying in the wilderness:
'Prepare the way of the Lord;
make his paths straight.'"
Now John wore a garment of camel's hair and a leather belt around his waist, and his food was locusts and wild honey.

October 20

¹Psalm 18:30

This God — his way is perfect;
the word of the Lord proves true;
he is a shield for all those who take refuge in him.

October 21

[1] 1 Corinthians 1:27

But God chose what is foolish in the world to shame the wise; God chose what is weak in the world to shame the strong.

October 22

[1] Proverbs 16:9

*The heart of man plans his way,
but the Lord establishes his steps.*

[2] Ephesians 4:14

so that we may no longer be children, tossed to and fro by the waves and carried about by every wind of doctrine, by human cunning, by craftiness in deceitful schemes.

November 2

[1] Isaiah 1:18

*"Come now, let us reason together, says the Lord:
though your sins are like scarlet,
they shall be as white as snow;
though they are red like crimson,
they shall become like wool."*

November 10

¹Judges 6:11-12, 25

Now the angel of the Lord came and sat under the terebinth at Ophrah, which belonged to Joash the Abiezrite, while his son Gideon was beating out wheat in the winepress to hide it from the Midianites. And the angel of the Lord appeared to him and said to him, "The Lord is with you, O mighty man of valor."

That night the Lord said to him, "Take your father's bull, and the second bull seven years old, and pull down the altar of Baal that your father has, and cut down the Asherah that is beside it."

December 2

¹1 Timothy 4:7-8

Rather train yourself for godliness; for while bodily training is of some value, godliness is of value in every way, as it holds promise for the present life and also for the life to come.

December 12

¹Jeremiah 2:23-24

How can you say, 'I am not unclean, I have not gone after the Baals'? Look at your way in the valley; know what you have done — a restless young camel running here and there, a wild donkey used to the wilderness, in her heat sniffing the wind! Who can restrain her lust? None who seek her need weary themselves; in her month they will find her.

December 14

[1] Chronicles 13:8

And David and all Israel were celebrating before God with all their might, with song and lyres and harps and tambourines and cymbals and trumpets.

December 28

[1]Song of Solomon 2:16

My beloved is mine, and I am his;
he grazes among the lilies.

February 20

[1]John 15:5

I am the vine; you are the branches. Whoever abides in me and I in him, he it is that bears much fruit, for apart from me you can do nothing.

March 10

[1]Luke 7:37-38

And behold, a woman of the city, who was a sinner, when she learned that he was reclining at table in the Pharisee's house, brought an alabaster flask of ointment, and standing behind him at his feet, weeping, she began to wet his feet with her tears and wiped them with the hair of her head and kissed his feet and anointed them with the ointment.

[2]John 13:23

One of his disciples, whom Jesus loved, was reclining at table [in the bosom of Jesus].

March 14

[1]Luke 10:42

"But one thing is necessary. Mary has chosen the good portion, which will not be taken away from her."

March 26

[1]Psalm 1:3

*He is like a tree
planted by streams of water
that yields its fruit in its season,
and its leaf does not wither.
In all that he does, he prospers.*

May 20

[1]Colossians 1:17

And he is before all things, and in him all things hold together.

[2]Ephesians 3:11-12

This was according to the eternal purpose that he has realized in Christ Jesus our Lord, in whom we have boldness and access with confidence through our faith in him.

July 20

[1]Psalm 26:2

Prove me, O Lord, and try me; test my heart and my mind.

July 23

[1]2 Corinthians 12:10

For the sake of Christ, then, I am content with weaknesses, insults, hardships, persecutions, and calamities. For when I am weak, then I am strong.

July 24

[1]Ecclesiastes 1:2 (NIV)

"Meaningless! Meaningless!" says the Teacher. "Utterly meaningless! Everything is meaningless."

August 8

[1]Matthew 11:28

"Come to me, all who labor and are heavy laden, and I will give you rest."

²Ecclesiastes 1:9

What has been is what will be, and what has been done is what will be done, and there is nothing new under the sun.

³Isaiah 41:18

I will open rivers on the bare heights, and fountains in the midst of the valleys. I will make the wilderness a pool of water, and the dry land springs of water.

⁴Psalm 4:1

Answer me when I call, O God of my righteousness! You have given me relief when I was in distress. Be gracious to me and hear my prayer!

August 9

¹Psalm 22:11

Be not far from me, for trouble is near, and there is none to help.

August 26

¹Galatians 5:1

For freedom Christ has set us free; stand firm therefore, and do not submit again to a yoke of slavery.

September 1

¹James 4:8

Draw near to God, and he will draw near to you.

September 2

[1]Philippians 4:13

I can do all things through him who strengthens me.

[2]Ephesians 6:14-18

Stand therefore, having fastened on the belt of truth, and having put on the breastplate of righteousness, and, as shoes for your feet, having put on the readiness given by the gospel of peace. In all circumstances take up the shield of faith, with which you can extinguish all the flaming darts of the evil one; and take the helmet of salvation, and the sword of the Spirit, which is the word of God, praying at all times in the Spirit, with all prayer and supplication.

[3]James 4:7

Resist the devil, and he will flee from you.

[4]Jeremiah 29:13

You will seek me and find me, when you seek me with all your heart.

September 3

[1]1 John 1:5

This is the message we have heard from him and proclaim to you, that God is light, and in him is no darkness at all.

September 7

[1]Psalm 73:26

My flesh and my heart may fail, but God is the strength of my heart and my portion forever.

September 8

[1]Ezekiel 37:11

Then he said to me, "Son of man, these bones are the whole house of Israel. Behold, they say, 'Our bones are dried up, and our hope is lost; we are indeed cut off.'"

September 17

[1]Ephesians 2:8

For by grace you have been saved through faith. And this is not your own doing; it is the gift of God.

September 22

[1]Matthew 8:26-27

And he said to them, "Why are you afraid, O you of little faith?" Then he rose and rebuked the winds and the sea, and there was a great calm. And the men marveled, saying, "What sort of man is this, that even winds and sea obey him?"

September 25

[1]James 1:17

Every good gift and every perfect gift is from above, coming down from the Father of lights with whom there is no variation or shadow due to change.

September 27

[1]Matthew 18:3

"Truly, I say to you, unless you turn and become like children, you will never enter the kingdom of heaven."

October 7

[1]1 John 4:18

There is no fear in love, but perfect love casts out fear.

October 8

[1]Philippians 2:13

For it is God who works in you, both to will and to work of his good pleasure.

[1]Ephesians 2:4-5

But God, being rich in mercy, because of the great love with which he loved us, even when we were dead in our trespasses, made us alive together with Christ — by grace you have been saved.

[1]Colossians 2:13

And you, who were dead in your trespasses and the uncircumcision of your flesh, God made alive together with him, having forgiven us all our trespasses.

October 10

[1]Prayer of St. Francis

October 13

[1]James 4:13-14

Come now, you who say, "Today or tomorrow we will go into such and such a town and spend a year there and trade and make a profit" — yet you do not know what tomorrow will bring. What is your life? For you are a mist that appears for a little time and then vanishes.

October 26

[1]Psalm 139:5

You hem me in, behind and before, and lay your hand upon me.

October 27

[1]John 10:10

The thief comes only to steal and kill and destroy. I came that they may have life and have it abundantly.

Dear Kickstarter backers,
this book would not exist without you:

Albert Cheung	Jon Kwan
Albert Zhou	Joy Chen
Alex and Caroline Shea	Junwen Feng
Alex Barker	Justin and Patricia Ho
Alexander Hong	Karen Lai
Alvin and Carmen Liew	Kenny Lin
Alyson Hau	Lana Norris
Andrea Yu	Larry M
Andrew Chou	Lawrence Wong
Andrew and Irene Li	Louise van der Meulen
Ashley and Carly Byrd	Manley Leung
Brian and Emilie Siu	Margo Chan
Brian Lo	Matt and Halley Anne Curtis
C M Crosby	Mei Mei Yip
Catherine Ngai	Michelle Cee
Cheryl Pong	Nadia Suen
Christine Chen	Norman Leung
Christopher and Diane Walker	Paul Cho
Christopher Changchien	Paul Measor
Christopher Choi	Pauline Au
Daniel Teoh Yong Liang	Queenie Lau
David Chui	Rachel Nam
Deborah Measor	Renee Chu
Derek and Emilie Worthington	Roger Rinesmith
Douglas McPherson	Simone Hui
Edina Choo	Stephen Michelle Caldwell
Elissa Scott	Steve Lee
Ellen Sevigny	Tara Vandermeer
Emma Wang	Terrance and Agatha Leung
Evelyn Ngeow	Tim Peierls
Giles Gibbins	Tony and Jenny Measor
Greg Wong	Tracy Foster
Helen Kim	Victor Tsang
Irene Chen	Vivian Sin
Janice Chua	Weston and Megan Ver Steeg
Jeff Leung	William and Yvette Shin
John and Ruth Chou	Yee Choi
Jon Cicoski	